As Meaning Returns

jules evans

BookLeaf
Publishing

India | USA | UK

Presentation by *BookLeaf Publishing*

Web: www.bookleafpub.com

E-mail: info@bookleafpub.com

ISBN: 9789360941383

First edition 2024

The Light that Echoes

I think that when I'm old and grey and the
teenager intimacies we share seem so far away,
I'll still write about you. Every poem is a sun
bear is a strawberry is a quaking aspen is a
cloud, which is to say every poem is an organic
thing, same long breath pushing out and against
the world, light pulsating unbearably.

Picture a warm summer evening, sun etching its
words onto your skin. I heard love was a
promise, & this is a summer evening you'd
particularly like: the wind kissing your ears and
your body swaddled in a tree's shadow, fading
light sifting through tuscan yellow leaves.
Maybe your hand is burning up against the palm
of someone you love. Maybe you are looking
out into the city, at the shimmering landscape,
listening to Leonard Cohen, wondering how this
is all happening to you, how you're happening to
it. Maybe the sky breaks with stars and mercy, a
poem lifting itself off the ground and into the
world like it was there all along. And maybe it
was, if you knew where to look, or how to listen
for it.

This particular evening I've been telling you about, it doesn't care that it's commonplace. The forest, the stardust, the birds, the planets, the moon—it's all been done before. It'll all be done again. Instead, it says: I'll do it as long as it keeps me from crawling out of this world. I'll do it as long as it makes life livable. As long as it is there, this light we bear witness to.

Deer-Hearted Year

Somewhere visible, backlit, cicadas hushing and
you, bone-tired,
too soft to perceive. We never left mid-August,
did we, some late summer
snowglobe fracturing to a gentleness in your
palms in spacious
seconds, misty through the spore-spackled glass,
blistering white sky.
I would have followed you anywhere, fabric
fluttering, fingertips wound and
smothering your wrist, joints against joints, bird
bones against life lines.
And when you smiled, all substance and light,
graves full of de-pitted fruit
dissipating to nothing, an open wound that
festered, bled, never healed. Knife
to flesh to the blend of every thought and every
receding horror, clambering, jagged
geography like braille. It's late November and if
I stepped into it I think I'd be swallowed up.

I knew then, like I've always known. Eyes
flickering like a storm, breath hollowing
out, swimming through deep, ugly, affected
silence, entry wounds over exit

wounds over open fractures. And here, shadows
illusory and shifting like some kind
of prison. You wished this world extinct, and
then it was. Negative space creasing
between cloud and fog, all falling action,
collapsing onto shoulders, always burdened,
always blurred. Now it's April, first warm day of
spring. You're eating strawberries like
you never left and my heart is a star-studded
ocean. Wishing you'd open your arms
and let me in. Wishing I'd told you how I felt
before you knew I was burning away.
Maybe this time you'll stay. Maybe this time. I
open my eyes, waiting, waiting.

Moonlit Breath

I'd give you the bigger half, lose at the
wish-bone, let the fruit
grow mould and not say a word simply because
you asked.
It's not decorum, keeping the grocery store
receipts, orange
juice just down the hall in the fridge. There's no
use pretending:
it's what we do, what we've always done,
running through the
backlit streets, hearts flayed open, something
tender and bright
growing between us like a bruise. No polite
exits. I'd keep you here
the whole time if you let me. The glass is empty
on the counter, dishes
piling up in the kitchen sink, laughter echoing
down the hall, and there's
comfort in that, in knowing I'll wake up
tomorrow and it'll still be here,
fully formed and wonderful, even if it's light
years away, even if I can't see it.

Pressure Point

i'd like to swap bodies with someone else, with someone you don't just love but like very much. is that selfish? i'm not the same person i was at thirteen but i don't think that's something you'd understand. i'm clawing at the light like a toddler and i think one day you'll notice me but you never do. you're the biggest man i know. i'm sorry. the pavement is littered with ash and a third of the sky's gone dark and there are only stars, falling silently, cardboard boxes gathering dust in the attic. i'm crying and a bit lacking all over and it's only ever white noise. anyway, you made light work of it, took something tender and made it messy, raw, prized knife, prized possession, same old semantic field, same old letters burning into the edges of my coffee cup. call it pride, or obsession. call it hurt. jars filling with rotten pickles, limbs grown to the point of no return. it's when i feel terribly sad that i don't vet every confession, that it spills onto the page like guts, like vomit. what i really want to say to you is that i've made something of myself & it's fine if you don't see it. but when i came back all i did was collapse, ground giving way beneath my feet, bones left to dry, ceramic plate

unwashed. i'm not sure what to make for dinner.
in dreams you call and i follow, reaching for
something, some proof that you were here and
you loved me and some of it mattered. & when
something shifts and everything goes dark like a
graveyard i remember that i love you but i don't
think i'll come to your funeral after all. i won't
return until i've found it, what i was looking for,
my lamb heart, red as youth. i'll never be whole
but i'll never be you, either. fast forward and i'm
twenty and the walk home is lovely and the stars
are beautiful and nothing is wrong with me or
ever was. sometimes growing older is knowing
when to stop believing. the night is warm on my
collarbones and my hand isn't empty, and my
childhood is devastatingly over but at least the
shadows are gone. & now the butterflies are
singing something blue and the future is a
golden stretch of road that goes on for miles and
miles and i still don't know what to make for
dinner but it's okay. it'll do.

Miles Away, Far into the Future

this is what happens to words said one too many
times, bleak, static,
always that little bit off, always that little bit
bruised. it's a long way down
and you don't remember the way back, tracing
firelit maps with your thumb,
dreaming up a world where everything's light
and the space where hurt
festers, bleeds, wounds doesn't exist, dissipates
to smoke, fog, nothing. if you
repeat something enough it becomes true. look,
bird bones scraped between
cobble, skeletons rattling in the attic. it only
means what you let it. & you've
tried everything: manhole covers, magic, lottery
tickets going nowhere. almost
everything, that is. overgrown and worn out,
stumbling like a weed, suffocating
in their grasp, twisting, arching, viper
swallowing its own flicking tail. here's
something beautiful you'll never touch again.
you know love only as they
gave it, not freely, only beautiful in its aftermath.
in their eyes you'll always

be a caricature. so what. swallow it, discard it,
let yourself into a room full of
what loves you, lock the door. take a flight to
san francisco, japan, anywhere.
stay away from the stove. it burns & you learnt
that the hard way. let the rain
tell you its story, cold and steady. tell it yours.
don't leave out the sun, the steps,
the warmth of your skin, your blood singing.
grocery store heart in your hands.
listen, they were wrong about you. they were
wrong. inhale, exhale. say it again.

Magnification

It's not a terrible secret. We're driving, great
highways glittering like
stars, heaven placed down upon the windshield.
Tempered April,
summer sun inevitably turning the space
between your shoulder
blades into something holy, something neither of
us dare to say
aloud. Your palm, hesitant, flat against my knee.
And everything
quiet, or maybe not, maybe it's just us, you
tucking your dragonfly
wings in, translucent and veined, me trying and
failing to find the
right words to say. Less of a girl and more of an
awkward, clutching
thing. I open my mouth and try again because I
know how much you
like to hear it, even without being asked, even
without being told.
And I don't miss the way you smile—obvious,
like a peeled
clementine, like the way my voice sounds when
I say your name.

So It Goes

There's nothing more humiliating than
the aftermath, than going out
   like a lightbulb in an ice storm,
globe flickering
once,
 twice, a third time,
 town square in my lily liver. Quit now while
you can, before it ends
the way most stories do.
     I would like to say that
I do not recognise you anymore.
  The truth: it is like looking into a mirror,
and pretending.
More memory than souvenir, stomach
dropping
 and everything rotten, spoiled, crawling with
insects,
so I haven't eaten, won't for a while. You and
me,
 we are telling the same story over and
over.
Don't you think it's getting old?
We could be something else. Me and you.
How easy it would be to forget.

                    The ways we fit inside
each other, the tarry lightless
salt-dark, your hand in mine.

Fever Dream Off the Estate

This is the place where all the hard lessons I've
learned finally make sense, where
I hold my hurt in my hands gently, turning
wound into water. I look in the
washed-up glass and don't see my mother, or the
self I was with her, or the self
I thought I'd become without. It all feels like a
mirror, waking up, every shadow
a half-written story begging to be forgiven. I
walk through my childhood without
shivering. I was always going to end up here, I
think. At the gaping mouth of a
garden, not wincing but still tender and blue,
like a frozen limb, like the soft space
between my elbows, beckoning the evening
light. I am no longer afraid of myself,
of what grows inside my bones. My skin is no
longer a costume, or a prison. And
how simple, how beautiful it feels, to be able to
reach out to a living thing without
flinching, to look at the world and not see fire,
or a body so easily consumed.

Postcard Poem

you miss her in light years, and there it is. your
long-tailed heart
fluttering home, home, and her. she's holding the
blue in her hands
and you're four again, coughing up a lung, a
kidney, your heart,
and there's strawberry jam on the walls where
they shouldn't be
and your bird skeleton splayed open on the floor,
brittle and bare.
(do you think that is love?)

you watch as she unlatches the shutters and the
light streams in
like a love affair, and this time, you don't
stumble, and you don't
feel locked in cement. think the moon, and her
tides. think quantum
entanglement, about how your atoms and her
atoms don't know you
were ever apart. your hands are bruised, but she
holds them anyway.
(do you think that is love?)

you're crawling out of a chrysalis, your eyes
unclosing, heavy as
water, carrying your body past the trees and into
the sky. are you getting
it now? you, a foreigner to yourself, to your own
decaying organs, to
the yellowed half-light whittling down the hours
and everything in
between, burning, burning. you want to tell this
story but you're going
nowhere. you're saying this, and this, and this;
you're baring your teeth,
leaking out half-blood half-sweet, and no one is
listening. no one is
looking. no one will ever look at you again.
(do you think that is love?)

it happens slowly, but it happens. the moon
rising above the stars, you rising with it.

Since I Do Love the World

it is not always winter here. the planet is full of
clouded water,
the river flowing uphill, the dogs running out,
their tongues pink
and flesh-bound like the sky, like the tulips
pressed up against
your palms. in my head you're all warm
bleeding heart and
thrumming fingertips that paint up pretty
dreamscapes stained
with grass and destiny and something much too
big for my chest and

i love you. i turn last saturday over and over like
a storybook page
and in between the salt-soaked sides of my
poetry i remember you,
and i remember the dying light against your
eyelids, and i remember
the milky way sprouting in my stomach like a
weed. nowadays my
arteries are clotted from heart to lung with blood
and fat, dizzy from
the comedown with mountain dew and sadness.
nowadays i leave

fingerprints everywhere i go, laugh into my
hands at the miracle that bursts from the
underside of my jaw. nowadays i think it's all i
have. the stars are sugar cubes in the
night sky and i'm wringing my hands to keep
from milking the moon so it pours talcum
light all over you like something holy,
something divine, and i can't stop thinking about
how i wanted to be something, then. about how i
wanted to be real, and whole, and
loved in a way that mattered, but it was going to
kill me. you were going to kill me.

Memoir

the loveseat is verdant green and one by one
you're winding parking lot
flowers around your thin-veined wrists, lifting
them to the fluttering streetlight,

and you're electric with it. in the midsummer
heat i whisper something secret
and you are all over my bed like a wine stain.
cherry pits everywhere, a frantic

clawing of hands, my teeth trapping in all the
words i want to say. i think i'll learn
how to pray for you. so what if you make me
laugh? so what if nobody holds a

candle to you? i won't love anyone else this way.
i'm alighting the train again,
heady and sick because i haven't dreamt the
ending, and my heart is aching and

my heart is a souvenir and above all my heart is
yours, and sometimes you live in drifting
apathy and we are asking each other what
forever really means. my sweet, do you

still have the key? there's water in my eyes and
my lungs and my lily liver and i'm waiting
for you to come home. and now the door is
swinging open. and the loveseat is still green.

Repetition

1

there it is, the gun, the barrel, the body.

which is to say the loneliness finally grew sick
in my bones,

because i wanted you alive
and i wanted and i wanted like anything good
could ever come out of wanting.
i held out my palms and asked what are you
holding on to?
and you said nothing, and i held out my palms
and said hold onto me and you
said nothing. there's something in that, in the
things we don't say, like the tide
turning in on itself, drowsy, sick, gleaming with
moonlight.

2

it's suicide, heart in your throat,
and the river is the road is the floorboards
beneath your mother's apartment

and you miss her so much your chest is sharp
with it, with memory
that moves and wrestles and fills your lungs with
water,
with rain, with the tears she usually saves for
you,

when she looks at you and sometimes all she can
do is
cry. but it's an impracticality, nothing
more, nothing less, so you let it sit in you, and
you
mother it and you think you understand
the difference between loving and being loved,
wanting
and being wanted. and there it is again, the gun,
the barrel, the body, which

is to say your mother never came to your funeral

and you're bleeding out but i remember the rain,
and i remember missing you.

3

i had a dream about you last night.
sorry about my hands, sorry about my heart,
sorry about my lungs.

i'm coughing up gasoline, choking on it, and i
think i could have loved you my entire life,
and i'm sorry. this time i'm the gun and i'm the
barrel and i'm the body
and every part of me is bright and wound, and
you say it's so lonely
here without you and i almost believe it. this
time our mosquito bite
summer doesn't end, and we keep swallowing
the same sticky-sweet
blueberries that press purple stains onto our skin,
and we
keep telling each other things we'll never
say again, and i keep wanting as much as i can
bear it.
this time, there are three consonants, and five
vowels, and you think
maybe the world is built on that. you know it is.

To Be Exact

i am learning to claw at the light
in the same way that it is learning to bleed
quietly, a shadow-fingered sliver of moonlight
sluicing holes through the floorboards.
remember, love folds oceans and oceans carry
love.
and likewise, your heart is a lighthouse, splitting
foam
and gleaming star-wine and shifting planes
wrung
and wrestled and wrangled into warmth,
weaving
worlds in the darkness between passing ships.
& you know how much i want to be the only
good
thing for miles but in dreams i'm always
apologising,
always sorry because i don't know how to be
good
without first being loved, and i don't know how
to be loved
without first being sorry. with every inhale my
chest cracks
in hollow breaths, and i carve it into my wrists
like a raw

rictus grin. i'm sorry, sweetheart. we both know nothing lasts
forever, but look how its light remains long after it's gone.

On Colour Theory

i had a dream about us last night.
me, gutted, coughing up
gasoline, you holding the match.
there's half a pomegranate in my
hands like spilled blood,
sweet as mahogany-crimson
and the winter-whittled ache inside
my bones. i almost tell you what
i think it means but some
words are better left untouched and
it's muscle memory, anyway,
wine-dark kisses in the
summer and the four bottles
of coke in the backyard, the moon
drifting a little further from the
earth each year, the guilt. in
between impulses i take
your hand because you're a
forest fire and i'm the
forest and you know i'd
go up in flames for you. but
i had a dream about us
last night, and you know how
that one goes.

Sixteen and Everything Else

it's late and no one goes to bed and our eyes are
strained open like that night with the
guitar, and the books. it's late and i'm twelve
again, falling through the cracks in the ceiling,
chest splitting apart with plastic stars and the
ache of missing it, of missing you. if we were
myth and memory, you'd be myth, i'd be
memory. not thirteen anymore but still all limb,
our laughter stuttering through the trees, crushed
flowers sickeningly sweet, pouring out of
the light. you, smiling, real again, not a fever
dream. what is it? i love you, i want you for the
world, i love you, there's no one else, i love you.
nothing. now, the dark scattered with
stars, scuff marks on the vinyl floor. now, the
worst gift in the world. now, my heart swollen,
turning over like a bad tooth, aching like a
broken bone.

last night we stood on the porch, wild
blackberries growing out back, and i couldn't
see the
stars at first but they came to me, winking into
existence above the streetlamps with every

blink, with every shutter of my eyelids. healing
is a little like that; you don't see it at first, but
our bodies are always mending, always stitching
themselves anew. you look at the skies, i
look at you. on the way we pick up souvenirs,
dented cardboard boxes, the road, deep
green everywhere. sixteen and in high school,
thinking maybe it'll last forever. we know it
won't.

(we buy the house six months later, paint the
walls white, put vases on the windowsills with
flowers in them that inevitably die because
neither of us can garden, heartbeats pulsing
lightly against our stomachs. everything crawls
out after, and we sit, and we talk, and we
don't, termites from woodwork. how did we get
here? you want to know. luck, i say,
thinking of something else entirely.)

Marilyn, for Mary

why aren't you going?
it's the only thing they ever ask, like they've
forgotten how to say anything else, like he
matters more than the girl they put into the
ground, all slight and lovely with jupiter's
moons for eyes. they drape six fresh
long-stemmed red roses over her casket that spill
over
her the same way her blood once did, pinholes
swallowing light and shards of shattered
glass and broken thumbs. when they ask, he says
it makes him sick, the wooden overcoat
and the affair and the whole lot of them,
weeping murderers who remind him of marble
sculptures and le génie du mal. it's not a lie, not
entirely, not yet.
he's an open wound without her, leaking alcohol
and adhesive tape, pulling bodies from
the wreckage. he's the only person she ever
really trusted, their bodies always together, her

hands bleeding warm light onto his. he thinks
there's something in that, in her whittled-
down pulse and the setting sun going back and
forth, but he doesn't know what. he doesn't

know anything anymore, and he doesn't know if
he ever will. he's still trying to piece
together the remnants of their lives, to figure out
how it all fit, once, how a love like theirs
ever went cold, but he doesn't know. he doesn't
know.
they talk, as most people do. they say he was
just killing time, nothing more, nothing less,
and she was anna and he was karenin and she
never saw the train coming. he doesn't
bother because it isn't worth it and he doesn't
believe in justifying himself to a room of
strangers who weren't around to see the way he
looked at her, back when she was alive and
thought love was something that filled rooms,
like floods or bees. she never realised love
could be quieter, that sometimes it was just
someone who kept on looking. it's too little,
too late, her bicycle collecting dust for forty
years she didn't get, his hands sickly with
flowers, three times a week, forever, a burst of
whirling light in his garage. he lets them talk,
tells them he's not going because he doesn't love
her, wonders vaguely how many lies
someone can tell before they get caught.
and all of it is the cricket bat slamming into the
back of his head, the stitches, his son crying,

blows for every discrepancy in his life. in his
head he breaks her thumb a million times, he
gets turned away, she keeps on crying. he never
figures her out and she tries to kill herself.
mary buys him malted milk and leaves. she
swallows the pills, tells him it's his fault. he
doesn't show up at her funeral. everyone asks
him the same question, over and over, black
blossoming on his eyes and in his stomach, like
it's the only thing they've ever wanted to
know. why aren't you going? this time he
laughs, swallows, opens his mouth. they ask him
why and it keeps happening. cut him open and
it's all so simple. she won't be there.

Momentarily Gentle & Gun-Coloured

she stands out like a gunshot and there are
stitches all over you to keep your heart from
spilling out, stitches you rip apart because it's
midnight and you're aching for her to see
you, to know you. it's dark out, more blue than
black, the yellowing light of the diner gone,
the sidewalk no longer covered in chalk. you are
the only two people in the universe who
exist and she's growing on you, a terrible rash,
promising you'll be something else,
something more. you understand, don't you? she
asks, her voice synonymous with
tenderness, like you could ever say no to her,
like you would ever want to. you think about
how you can almost reach the stillborn stars with
your fingers outstretched, about her at the
doorway, saying let's stay here forever. you're
there on the carpet, worrying about the cord,
the tangles, legs tucked firmly beneath you.
you're there on the carpet, dying to know what
she meant by forever, by the promise of
countless sunsets and deathbeds and the brilliant
blue of a butterfly's wings, there and there and
then gone. and in the entire scope of the

universe you're hardly important but she's a star
in the daytime, which is to say you love
her, which is to say your heart is a chunk of
blood in between your ribs, eleven times too
small for this. which is to say the world is made
of light and she isn't so much the sun but
the entire cosmos, the milky way rooted in her
nerves like cancer, or flowers. which is to say
she's neptune and you're burning up in her orbit
and you think of pretty houses and the
two of you in them until you decompose into the
carpet and someone scrubs you away,
and it aches a little because you don't know
what you'd do without her. months and months
and months later she gives you a piece of herself
and your head turns to water and your
heart turns into a fortress and it becomes a piece
of you, spreading everywhere like warm
dying sunlight, and there it is, finally: the two of
you, charred edges and leaking veins and
crackling static and a lonely flower garden
cloaked in silver.

Where I Was Leaving, Without You

in the clearing, in south-facing fields and unperturbed woods, in cleaved apart valleys that never level, the hunter lowers his bow. the aftermath is always worse, always violent, shuddering silence and bloodied ribs, stumbling blindly past pine forests, river birches sinking into bits of shadow. the entire world a mirror, deer skittering on muddied earth, eyes wild, shifting, smeared. you and your periwinkle flowers, your delicate palms broken open, slim-wristed and tender and biting into fibreglass, reaching, wanting, never whole. dawns turning into epilogues and dreams into contours, honey-heavy light reinventing itself somewhere in the glowing atrium of the world. silhouettes darkening into something dangerous, prying, unsure, the sky crimson above you, bleeding everywhere. everything a target, limp quiver sliding into place. it reminds you of a story that never ended, of where you were going without him. steady now, don't move. and at the last second, nothing.

he's never known where to aim, no matter which
way he turns, no matter how much he wants
something to show for it, bruised fingertips and
throat broken open, splayed. watching from afar,
never sinking his arrows. the hunter, the hunted.
(it's an old story they tell at bars, scratched into
burnished wood and rising above the clinking of
shining glass, variations emerging over the years
but always with the same premise: that there's a
person the hunter must kill, and there's a person
the hunter can never kill, and sometimes they're
the same person, and sometimes they're you.)
the lights wink out and you're desperate for an
opening, pulling him from the lake onto the
moss-ridden forest floor, heavy, water-logged in
the gloom, head full of the thames. you're a liar
and a traitor and he won't thank you for it but
you'd do it a second time. you would. lose the
world, if it meant saving him. & now, a long
stretch of quiet. now, love from a distance. now,
moonlight faltering, wire rim of his glasses
glowing a winter-blue so familiar.

the air swirls a sickly white and grey,
slow-moving, too silent for a moment that's so
obviously colossal. you wake, feverish, to the
sound of heavy footfalls breaking through grass,
clumsy, his. he's standing above you, or maybe
he isn't, maybe it's another trick of the light,

maybe you're just dreaming. three-quarters of a
raw, rictus grin, all cheekbones and eyelashes
and shattered bone-white porcelain, mask sliding
off a face you pretended to forget. going
somewhere without me? it's something of a
joke, but it comes out all wrong, almost drunken,
stupid thing to say. you catch yourself, swallow.
he says nothing, and closes his eyes. sorry, force
of habit. the quarter-moment passes, lit up like a
lightbulb, too honest, too pronounced. and along
the riverbend, a loom of water flooding your
vision, familiar quiet splash where he leaves.

you'd follow him anywhere. even like this,
confused, disoriented and shaken, you'd follow
him. most anywhere, that is. every entanglement
of your life and his melting quietly into a pale
stream, dissipating to silence, the blue beating,
the ground giving way beneath you, the wintry
skyline crumbling under your weight, breaking,
all at once, sleeve of ash falling off a lit
cigarette. you're stumbling through a mist
towards two twinkling spots that might be eyes,
or might be distant, earthbound stars, nothing
here but fields, and thickets, and ancient acacia
trees creating a little lattice of branches through
which the dying starlight sifts. the axe feels
heavy in your hands. your hands feel heavy
without it, without him.

you're dreaming again. this time, the whole
world is empty, everything soundless and waxy
like a silent movie. this time, there are flowers
lining your wrists, blood running up their stems,
an open field of wheat and barley in the hollow
of your palms. this time, he doesn't run when he
sees you, and you don't look at him like you're
sorry, and you still remember how to be brave.

he looks up, knees sprawled on the hardwood
floor, moss-green eyes dark and beautiful in the
cold cosmic light. you're aching to kiss him, but
don't, even though it pains you, because he's the
best thing you've ever had and you'd take
anything over ruining that, you'd take being
dead. the bed sits low to the ground, frame
bearing signs of rust, limp mattress worryingly
thin. the garish flowers are crushed, desiccated
in your palms. don't go, you say. it's selfish, out
in the open, but there's something in that, in the
sincerity bleeding through your chest, in the way
he stares at you, expression shuttering, like
you're something he can't quite wrap his head
around. it seeps through you, between bones,
becoming inseparable from everything else. your
mind has eked out the top of your head, as if it's
been bashed in. you can't describe how you feel
about him without it sounding violent. outside,

the rain hurls itself in sheets against the glass,
cold as concrete. inside, the pictures rattle in
their frames. you think about how they'll be
there in the morning. you think about how he
won't.

Taxidermy

you thought you'd be dead by now, but you're
still right where you grew up:
sitting cross-legged in the back of rooms, telling
secrets. your body smaller
then, flat against the vinyl wallpaper, not an easy
thing to hold, all bony
elbows and half-suggestions, never a complete
thought. your organs emptying
themselves, aching in all the right places, flesh
wound that becomes memory
that becomes a haunting. blink and you'll miss
it, pressing bloody knuckles to
your mouth, flash of antlers against the dense,
lightless trees, salt-stain glint
of red, of simmering silver, your mother's name
holding you under freezing water
like an unwanted child, always drowning,
always more ghost than girl in that same
fault line, same liminal space. preserving horrors
in jars, steel angels adorning
your collarbones, wrapped in opaque plastic.
back in dreams where healing
doesn't simmer, doesn't carve you into two, & i
meet you just at the mile radius and

it doesn't sting the way it did at the undertaker's.
both of us at the doorway, frozen
in limbo, your chipped tooth shining something
sinister. somebody's on the table,
dead man without breath, maybe the mortician,
maybe you. buck and bonesaw, more
daring when you're still. which is to say a house
fire is never gentle. which is to say
you never left the narrative, not even when i
pleaded, last lighted room filling itself
with horror after horror, still breathing, still
haunted, smoke curling through each
rotting floorboard. this is the part where you
offer to stay, because you never knew
how to spare me—taxidermy ricocheting like a
bullet tearing into softness, ripping open
layer after layer after layer. don't worry, it
doesn't matter. i wouldn't have felt a
difference even if it did. what matters is the end
scene, where you turn me inside out
just to prove i'm still alive. go ahead. it's a good
punchline. i'm sorry about the innards,
i really did love you once.

Space Asunder

I hear your sun-splitting laugh in the
marketplace and my
heart hauls itself up, de-pitted fruit bruised with
wanting. I have here
all the substance and matter of you: whirling
light granted
by the twin flames burning up against your
palm, warm and yearning
to cauterise flesh. A disruption in the space that
held you & no means of egress—

but I'll be brief, I don't have the words. I heaved
them into
my mouth like shovelling coal into a furnace,
shining film of
sweat clinging to the back of my neck, last gasp
of a fever.
I took your shape. I inherited this filth. I bite it
back down.
There's a curl of water-darkened hair plastered
to your cheek.
I reach out to touch it, withdraw, reach out.
The similes are gone and I'm down to just later
and maybe, this gun-coloured limbo,

this intensifying negative space where a decision
is never quite reached.

Forget about the gnashing teeth and the
punctured veins, call it
self-inflicted and lie there like a dead thing. The
hitch is that you'll never
be anything else. It shouldn't matter, but
remember it is who and where,
it is who and where you are. In the searing cold I
think: this time, hurt won't
be there. I think: the world will be quiet for
everyone I love.

Vantage Point

Here we are arranging fences around fences,
rain-swollen with remorse. Your bad news piling
up without
resolution, chronic condition crippling our
reprieve.
Every little surrender & my dragonfly heart.
The kitchen blade shining hotly, sweet with
blood, blackening bone and sinew.
Same sordid song you'll always be singing.

Sullen litany of life. Twilight wavering steadily
across the sidewalk. Where I was leaving you:
the salt-dark ocean, the quiet deepening of that
mercurial,
snowmelt expanse, almost as hazy as a dream
dissolving into wakefulness, sharp sound.
Light that surrenders, that doesn't go the whole
distance.
It winds up here, shining blue at its depths,
exhausted.

My lunary miracle, my northbound satellite.
You lived here once. I know. We're approaching
the end of the line

& I want to tell you something foreign; true
north, Ithaca.
The translation dying on my tongue, sour-stale.
You have to pay attention. From this vantage
point you can see
the guileless luminance of the stars, the honeyed
sunset
whittled down to an ache.
Brittle wind hurtling past highways & through
state lines.
Beauty carved into every crevice.
Nothing's lost forever.

Call me, sweetheart,
I'll let you be dead wrong this time.
We'll turn up wherever love is & write our
names in the guestbook.
Now, the curdled tealight on the windowsill
stitches our
wounds up, more tender than I remember.

www.ingramcontent.com/pod-product-compliance
Lightning Source LLC
Chambersburg PA
CBHW061728130726
47996CB00006B/2549